How to Take Your Pension Pot

A Practical Guide to Your Retirement Options

Nick Bamford

First edition published in Great Britain 2015

Copyright © 2015 by Nick Bamford

The rights of Nick Bamford to be identified as the author of this work have been asserted by him in accordance with the Copyright, Designs and Patents Act 1998.

ISBN: 978-1-326-14590-3

Typeset in Garamond

Informed Choice Chartered Financial Planners

Sundial House, 20 High Street,
Cranleigh,
Surrey, GU6 8AE
www.icfp.co.uk

The contents of this book do not constitute financial or other professional advice. You should consult your professional adviser if you require financial advice.

Contents

How to Take Your Pension Pot

A Practical Guide to Your Retirement Options

About the Author

Nick Bamford is a very experienced Chartered Financial Planner and was previous Chairman of the Society of Financial Advisers (SOFA).

He is an Associate of the Personal Finance Society (APFS). In 2006 he graduated from Napier University with a BA Honours degree in Financial Services.

Nick has been an independent Financial Planner since 1989. He has spent his entire working life in the financial services profession.

When he is not working he spends time with his wife Andy (who was joint creator of Informed Choice) and his five grandchildren. Or you will find him watching sport (Football and Rugby mainly) fishing or enjoying the countryside.

Chapter One
Introduction

Introduction

Take the stress out of your life.

Moving home, changing jobs, marriage and divorce are said to be amongst the most stressful of life events. Based on my experience I think we can safely add to that list, *making the right choices about your "pension pot" at retirement.*

Just why is it that taking benefits from your pension pot is such a stressful event? There are a number of reasons including, but not limited to;

- Confusion, particularly because the pensions industry is so fond of using jargon;
- Fear, that getting it wrong might result in a poorer financial future;
- A negative press around the way in which consumers are treated by the financial services industry;
- Cost, a concern that getting professional advice may be expensive;
- Too much choice, how do you work out which option is right for you?

Effective way to save for retirement

Whilst pension arrangements remain one of the most effective ways to save for retirement they are subject to an awful lot of rules and regulation.

In March 2014 The Chancellor of the Exchequer George Osborne announced some significant changes to the choices and options available to the "pension pot" owner.

Most of these changes take effect from April 2015. If you are about to decide what to do with your "pension pot" then I have written this book as a practical guide for you.

Pension pot

Throughout the book I have used the expression "pension pot" as a simple piece of shorthand to describe a money purchase (or defined contribution) pension plan.

Such plans are often comes with labels like Personal Pension Plan, Stakeholder Pension Plan, Self-Invested Personal Pension, Retirement Annuity or Occupational Money Purchase Pension Scheme.

Put simply, such a plan is an accumulated "pot" of money created by you from contributions paid into your plan in addition to which income tax relief has been added. Those monies were then invested for growth.

You may also have had employer contributions paid into your pot. In some cases you may have had rebates of the National Insurance contributions paid by you and your employer redirected into your pot as well.

In my view it is quite healthy to think of your pension plan (whichever type it is) as a "pot of money"; it is after all simply money that has been accumulated with some tax breaks. Don't be put off by the "pension" label.

The real challenge for you now, as you reach retirement, is what to do with your pension pot.

Avoiding jargon

Throughout the book I have tried to avoid jargon. There is some risk with this approach in that pension professionals may seek to challenge the completeness of the book. Frankly, I don't care.

This book isn't written for my peers, it is written for you the pension pot owner. I honestly believe that you will benefit from a plain English explanation rather than fill the book with unnecessary jargon.

As I said above one of the reasons this subject is a stressful event for many people is the jargon that is used by the financial services industry. Dozens of words that are used by the pensions industry are simply alien to the normal human being!

We can start the process of de-stressing your decision by doing away with jargon. For example, I have decided not to rely on a glossary of terms in this book. If I use a word that I think needs translating into normal language I will do that on the page where it appears.

I have, however, put a lot of information in the book about the shape of annuities. This is because I want you the reader to think of the annuity as a starting point for comparing your pension pot choices and options. An annuity is a financial device for converting your pension pot into a lifetime of income.

A myriad of questions

During my career as an independent Financial Planner I have always encouraged people to ask questions. This is a healthy thing to do; the more questions you ask the better the chances of you understanding what is right for you.

I have provided you with a myriad of questions. Those questions need to be asked of you, your pension plan provider and anyone from whom you take guidance or advice.

The book is a practical guide and it is designed to empower (buzz word, sorry) you and help you to make good choices about what to do with your pension pot.

Professional advice

I should say up front, if in doubt then do take professional, independent and impartial advice. I would say that, wouldn't I? Yes, but I mean it.

Taking advice from an authorised and regulated independent financial adviser can absolutely help to de-stress the experience. It can ensure that you make the right decisions. It can save you from making some very expensive mistakes indeed.

You may feel confident enough to do it all yourself and that is fine too.

Do not though be put off taking advice because you think it is costly. Paying for advice might well save you a lot of money in the future by preventing you making the wrong decision today.

Structure

I have structured the book in what I hope is a logical format;

The next chapter is **About You** and your needs, your wants and your attitude towards retirement benefits.

At the end of that chapter you will find 20 questions that you need to ask yourself. If you can answer those questions you will be well on the way to making the right choices at retirement.

About You is followed by **About Your Pension Pot.**

You may of course have more than one pension pot and in my experience people may have as many as six or more separate pension pots, usually as a result of job changes throughout their career.

Often those people will have started a new plan each time they changed jobs. You need to find out a lot about your existing plans because they may well contain some important benefits. This book will arm you with the right questions to ask of your pension pot provider.

You also need to consider how best to manage your various pension pots and I have included some commentary on the things that you need to consider if you choose to consolidate the plan monies that you have into a new plan ahead of taking money from your pension pot.

At the end of this chapter I have repeated the 20 questions you need to ask of your pension provider.

About Your Choices and Options is a plain English guide that will explain the choices and options available to you.

If there is anything that drives up the stress levels of a pension pot owner it is the confusion that lies in this area. Remember there are advantages and disadvantages to every financial decision that we make.

Advantages and disadvantages explains that, just because there are disadvantages it does not mean we should not take that course of action.

Even though a course of action may be advantageous it does not mean that we should ignore the disadvantages; they may come back to haunt us! For each choice I have provided a list of advantages and disadvantages.

One way of understanding the right choice for you is to consider how other people in similar circumstances to you have dealt with their choices and options. In the **Case Studies** section I take a look at some real life scenarios (but I have protected the identity of the actual persons involved).

Some of the case studies are an amalgam of client situations in order to describe to you why they took the action that they did take.

The chapter **About Guidance and Advice** is important because of the changes for 2015 introduced by the government. One of those changes is the introduction of the Guidance Guarantee service to be delivered face to face by the Citizens Advice Bureau (CAB) and over the phone by The Pensions Advisory Service (TPAS).

Guidance is a no cost service to the consumer (it is paid for by a levy on the financial services industry) but it is very different to advice. In this part of the book I explain the difference between guidance and advice.

"You should judge a man by his questions not by his answers" – Voltaire

I wanted this book to provide a really practical experience for the reader. If you can complete the answers to **The Questions** as you read your way through the book you will end up with a personal action plan that you can use to engage with an authorised and regulated financial adviser or instil some real confidence if you decide to do it for yourself.

As hard as it may be a very good starting point for the reader will be to try to calculate how much retirement income that they need. When clients approach me for advice they very often say things like "I need to sort out my pension plans". Over the years I have taught myself to hear a slightly different statement and that is "When can I afford to retire?"

Of course that question can really only be answered when we know how much retirement income is needed. **Your Retirement Budget** helps you to put down in one place what your anticipated spend in retirement is likely to be and it includes both the essentials and the discretionary spend that you might expect in retirement.

Whilst the focus of this book is on how to take your pension pot, in my experience it is often the case that people have additional retirement income that can be provided by various other resources.

Your Assets is a simple schematic that looks at the assets that you have that might produce additional retirement income, for example, ISA investments, cash accounts and state pension benefits. By working out a realistic amount of income that might be generated from these assets you can get an overall picture of your total retirement income.

I have concluded the book with **Your Action Plan**, a summary of the whole book and if you are able to complete this you will be in a very good position to make an informed choice about how to take the benefits from your pension pot.

Please enjoy the book

I hope you enjoy reading this book (I certainly enjoyed writing it) but more importantly I hope it takes some of the stress out the choices you have to make.

I have added lots of sub-headings to the copy in this book. I was talking to a client about writing this book and he suggested (thank you to Andrew Sykes) that one of the things that puts people off reading material like this is if there is too much copy and it isn't broken down into bite size chunks. I hope this structure helps the reader.

Do let me know what you think of the book how it might be improved or what else you think might be added to help the reader. You can email me at nick@icfp.co.uk and follow me on Twitter @nickbamford.

Chapter Two
About You

About You

Let's talk about you.

What do you want?

What do you need?

If you have a pension pot and want to convert your pot into retirement benefits (income and capital) it will pay you real dividends to have some robust answers to those two questions.

Arming yourself with the answers to the following questions will also help you to ensure that you make the right choices about what to do with your pot.

1. Do you need/want to take your pension benefits now, or can you defer taking them?

We often use the word retirement to mean taking the benefits from your pension pot but retirement usually means stopping work. Truth is you do not have to retire to take benefits from a pension pot.

You can continue to work *and* take your pension benefits.

It's possible that you might use the opportunity of taking your pension pot benefits now in order to reduce the amount of paid work that you do. In other words gradually move into retirement over time. So do you need to take the benefits right now?

It may be that you are thinking to yourself, "You know what, I have saved hard to accumulate this pension pot over many years and I *want* to enjoy the proceeds now". That is perfectly understandable.

2. Do you need/want to take your tax free cash lump sum (but without taking any income benefits)?

It is perfectly possible to take your entitlement to a tax free cash lump sum from your pension pot now, without using the rest of your pot to provide a retirement income. In fact doing this has become more and more popular over time.

This is particularly so as the post-war Baby Boomer generation works to help the next generation with such things as getting onto the housing ladder or maybe even starting their businesses.

It may be that you have some spending plans and the tax free cash is a convenient source of money. Or perhaps you have some debt and want to use the tax free cash to pay off that debt.

In any event, in many circumstances taking the tax free cash and investing it to generate income can be a tax efficient step to consider.

Of course if you take the tax free cash and spend it, give it away or use it to pay off debt you reduce the future value of your retirement income as a result.

3. What do you expect your cost of living to be each year?

Have you prepared a budget? It is important to work out what your bills are going to be in retirement but I accept that this can be a challenging thing to do.

Spending patterns in retirement are initially difficult to predict.

You may go through a typical profile of spending more in the early years straight after retirement but with a subsequent reduction in later years and then a further spending spike in much later life when, for example, care fees are required to be paid.

At the very least you might want to have a handle on what the regular bills are going to be such as energy and food and costs associated with housing.

Take a look at **Your Retirement Budget** towards the end of this book and see if you can start to prepare your retirement budget plan.

You may need to establish what those likely bills are now and factor in some inflation for the future. To an extent these are at best going to be guestimates of what the actual spend will look like, but still a worthwhile exercise.

4. What other income will you have in retirement?

It may well be that in addition to your pension pot you have other sources of retirement income. Depending upon your age you may be entitled to state pension benefits either immediately or later on.

On their own, state pension benefits generally don't provide a high level of retirement income. However, when this income is added together with your other financial resources it can make a significant difference to the quality of your retirement life.

You should find out about your state pension entitlement; visit www.gov.uk/state-pension-statement and obtain a state pension forecast.

Perhaps you have worked for a company in the past and were fortunate enough to be a member of an employer sponsored pension scheme, one where the benefits were based on a formula and known as a "defined benefits" or "final salary scheme" benefits. If you have had membership of such a pension scheme you will be entitled to a known pension amount per year.

Do you have money saved in a bank, building society or post office account?

If you do you may receive interest on those accounts that you can spend as income in retirement. Whilst interest rates at the present time are generally pretty "poor" it all adds up so make a note of how much income such accounts might generate.

You may have an investment portfolio of some type. Perhaps you invested in ISA accounts (cash ISAs for example) or Stocks and Shares ISAs invested in shares, fixed-interest stocks or even commercial property funds.

Or you have a general investment account perhaps invested in collective investment funds. Or even a share portfolio that might generate dividend income.

Each of those investment assets can be used to generate retirement income in addition to that from your pension pot, so now is a good time to try to work out how much income those investments might produce.

Some people have successfully invested in buy-to-let residential property portfolios and from that investment might receive rental income. This will also form part of their retirement income and can be added to any other sources of income they may have.

Take a look at **Your Assets** towards the end of this book which might help you to identify the current capital value of your assets and how much income you might receive from those assets.

5. Do you need to pay off any debt?

If you have debt (for example a mortgage or bank loan) this will put something of a dampener on your ability to enjoy retirement and it makes sense to consider paying it off either before you retire or possibly with your tax free cash lump sum.

Examine the interest rates that you are paying on any debt that you have and good practice will be to pay off debt that is incurring the highest interest rate, this is a drain on your retirement income.

If you have a mortgage your mortgage lender may well be expecting you to repay it when you retire. If your tax free cash is insufficient to discharge all your debt then you are going to need to have a plan of action to service that debt from your retirement income so it should be included in **Your Retirement Budget**.

6. Do you need to make provision for a surviving spouse/partner on your death?

If you have a spouse or partner who is financially dependent upon you then you may need to arrange your pension pot benefits such that in the event of your death income or capital continues to be paid to them.

If on the other hand your spouse/partner will have sufficient financial resources to live the life that they want, after your death, without any benefits from your pension pot, you may have greater flexibility in how you arrange your own pension benefits.

7. Do you want to make money available to your survivors in the event of your death?

Do you have children or grandchildren to whom you would want to leave your pension pot in the event of your death?

If you do then this will also be an important factor to consider in arranging your own retirement income. How much do you want them to receive and should that money come from your pension pot or from other financial resources?

8. Do you require any flexibility in the amount and timing of your retirement income?

Many people want the absolute certainty of the income that they are going to receive from their pension pot.

Others have an eye on the future, perhaps they are some years away from receiving state pension benefits or pension income from an ex-employer's pension scheme. Or even expect to inherit a sum of money. They might wish to have some income now but a reducing amount in the future when those other benefits become payable.

Alternatively they may want to consider some forward tax planning perhaps anticipating a substantial capital gain from disposing of investments and therefore reducing their income tax rate might be beneficial.

Or they may know that they are going to inherit in the future and can afford to spend more now but have a need for less income later on.

9. Do you need a guaranteed income for the rest of your life?

Certainty of income can certainly be a great stress remover!

It may also be that you are risk averse and don't really like the prospect of the volatility that comes from investing your pension pot to generate income. You may have a known set of retirement bills and need your pension pot to cover those costs.

If you are risk averse and need a guaranteed income then there are ways to convert your pension pot into a guaranteed stream of gross monthly income for the rest of your life ("gross", because the income tax payable on pension income is subject to change and thus the net income might change from year to year).

10. Do you need a guaranteed income for the life of your partner/ spouse?

It may well be that not only do you need a guaranteed stream of gross retirement income but so does your surviving spouse or partner in the event of your death.

Or it may be that you can personally tolerate a variable amount of retirement income but your surviving spouse needs guaranteed income in the event of your death. You need to consider these potentially conflicting requirements.

11. What is your attitude towards and appetite for investment risk and reward?

Different ways of converting your pension pot into retirement income will have different degrees of investment risk associated with them. There is something of a trade-off between risk which might deliver greater ultimate benefits and guarantees which might provide lower overall benefits, but absolute certainty of income during your lifetime.

You need to establish your attitude to investment risk. Consider your experiences of investing during your lifetime (both the positive and negative experiences).

What did you learn from those experiences? Do you have a good understanding of the relationship between risk and reward?

Professional advisers will typically use an approach based around asking you a whole series of psychometric questions. These are designed to get a good overall understanding of your risk attitude.

The adviser will then discuss their findings with you to establish a risk label for you. They will then use that label to aid any investment portfolio modelling and portfolio construction that is needed for your pension pot.

This is though just a starting point. When it comes to investing pension pots we are all different and investing our pension pot should be about a bespoke approach for each person.

12. During your retirement what capacity do you have for any investment loss?

If any investments you make with your pension pot were to fall sharply in value what impact would that have on your capacity to have the retirement lifestyle that you want?

For some people *any* reduction in the value of their pension pot might represent an unacceptable outcome. This might even be true if they were to leave the money invested long enough and eventually the money was to recover its value.

Other people have greater tolerance for fluctuating capital and income values, particularly if they have other sources of retirement income to support them.

13. Do you have any medical conditions or lifestyle habits (smoking for example) that might potentially shorten your life expectancy?

One of the challenges that the pension pot owner is faced with is that of estimating his or her life expectancy.

Actuarial professionals produce tables that demonstrate the average expectancy of life for men and women of various ages who are living in the UK. But these are averages and remember you are not a number!

If you have a medical condition or a history of ill-health it may be that you have a reduced expectancy of life.

Strangely, this can be beneficial when it comes to converting your pension pot into income. If you choose to buy a financial instrument known as an "annuity" (more of that later). You might get a higher income because of your health. It might also influence your decision about how to take your pension pot if you are keen to pass on capital to the next generations.

14. What will you do if you spend your pension pot too quickly and run out of money later on?

If you do not convert your pension pot into a guaranteed income for life then you are going to have to manage your pension pot and make sure that it does not run out before you die.

What will you do if it does? Most people don't have a plan B so they need to be pretty sure that plan A is going to work.

15. Do you feel confident enough to make your own retirement decisions or do you need advice?

It is perfectly possible for the pension pot owner to decide exactly what they are going to do with their money and execute whatever transactions are necessary. The power of the Internet makes this absolutely doable.

There are many sources of information and guidance available to the pension pot owner. But be aware, as well as a good source of information the internet is also a quite brilliant source of disinformation!

If you take advice then you receive a great degree of consumer protection that you don't get if you DIY it. The role of the adviser as you will see later is to de-stress the lives of their clients.

16. What impact will inflation have on the value of your retirement income?

Inflation erodes the value of money. It is generally not too noticeable in the short term but over longer periods of time it will seriously damage the value of your retirement income. What rate of future inflation are you factoring into your plans?

Do not ignore inflation it has become the real enemy of many retired people and you and I are no different to many millions who have gone before us.

17. Are you prepared to pay more income tax now, to access your pension fund?

When the freedom and choice in pension changes were announced they were greeted with a good deal of excitement and enthusiasm. After all, the Chancellor's announcement was that people would never again have to buy an annuity with their pension pot and could take the whole of their pot as a lump sum. (Despite the fact that the compulsory purchase of an annuity with a pension pot disappeared some years ago!)

Then of course along came the realisation that only the first 25% of the pot was tax free. The rest of the pension pot would be subject to income tax at 20%, 40% or even 45%.

So, are you prepared to pay a big chunk of your pension pot to HMRC as income tax in order to access the rest of it today? Big decision time.

18. If you do take all your pension pot benefits now as a lump sum what are you going to do with those monies?

Spend it all now? Give it away (to the children and grandchildren) save it or invest it?

The freedom and choice in how you use your pension pot also comes with some important responsibilities because you are going to have to make your decisions in an imperfect world, with imperfect data and it is not going to be easy.

You will need to examine all your choices and options to determine what is right for you and your family and you may well need professional help from a qualified, experienced, authorised and regulated adviser.

19. How long do you expect to live?

If I ask you for your date of birth you will give me an answer pretty quickly.

If I ask you for your date of death however, you will almost certainly not be able to give me a precise date.

You will need to think about your life expectancy quite a lot because you will have to ensure that you don't run out of pension pot money too soon.

Most people significantly underestimate their life expectancy.

20. Do you understand all of the choices and options available to you?

You have a number of choices and you need to have real understanding not only of how those choices and options work but which ones are going to be most suitable to fulfil your needs and wants. Indeed some of them will be totally unsuitable for you and you will need to avoid them.

Write down your answers to these questions. You may not have all those answers ready yet so we have repeated these questions at the end of this chapter so that you can return to them later.

About You – The Questions

1. Do you need/want to take your pension pot benefits now, or can you defer taking them?

2. Do you need /want to take your tax free cash lump sum (but without taking any income benefits)?

3. What do you expect your cost of living to be each year?

4. What other income will you have in retirement?

5. Do you need to pay off any debt?

6. Do you need to make provision for a surviving spouse/partner on your death?

7. Do you need to make money available to your survivors in the event of your death?

8. Do you require any flexibility in the amount and timing of your retirement income?

9. Do you need a guaranteed income for the rest of your life?

10. Do you need a guaranteed income for the life of your spouse/partner?

11. What is your attitude towards and appetite for investment risk and reward?

12. During your retirement what capacity do you have for any investment loss?

13. Do you have any medical conditions or lifestyle habits (smoking for example) that might potentially shorten your life expectancy?

14. What will you do if you spend your pension pot too quickly and run out of money later on?

15. Do you feel confident enough to make your own retirement decisions or do you need advice?

16. What impact will inflation have on the value of your retirement income?

17. Are you prepared to pay more income tax now to access your pension pot?

18. If you do take all your pension pot benefits now as a lump sum what are you going to do with all those monies?

19. How long do you expect to live?

20. Do you understand all of the choices and options available to you?

Chapter Three
About Your Pension Pot

About Your Pension Pot

You will need to find out a good deal of information about your pension pot. You should receive, ahead of the selected retirement date for your pension, a wake-up package of information from your pension plan provider.

The wake-up package might consist of many pages of information and figures. Some providers will send to you in excess of twenty pages of notes and figures. You may well find that this is a barrier to action—don't let it be!

The information that you receive, in particular the illustrations that are sent to you by your pension pot provider, may not be personalised and specific to your circumstances.

For example, your pension pot provider may not be aware of such basic things as your current state of health or your health history or whether you have a spouse or partner. If you do have a spouse or partner they may well not know their date of birth.

The wake-up pack may well contain some valuable information, but it might also be difficult to understand and confusing.

You should ask your pension plan provider the following questions. If you use the services of a professional adviser they will ask these questions of your pension pot provider for you.

1. What is the current value of my pension plan?

The current value of your pension pot will be an important factor in determining the total amount your retirement benefits. It is though not necessarily a guaranteed figure it might be subject to change (see below).

When you know the value of your pot you will be able to work out approximately how much tax free cash lump sum is available to you.

2. Is this the value available to me if I decide to take the benefits now, either from you or another provider?

Sometimes the current value of your pension pot and the value available to you to provide benefits are different. Typically the latter figure is lower.

This might be the case if you are retiring earlier than the selected retirement age under your plan. Effectively the pension pot provider is taking from the current value the plan the charges that they would have taken over the term to the selected benefit age.

You will have to decide if paying this penalty is worthwhile in order to receive benefits now.

In some instances the current value quoted by the plan provider is lower than the amount available to you to buy your retirement benefits.

This might be the case where your pension plan is invested in a with-profits fund where there is a terminal bonus be paid by the plan provider.

If such a bonus is being paid it is well worth while considering taking the value of your plan as such a bonus might be lower than the current quoted figure or actually none at all, in the future.

3. Can the quoted value of my pension plan fall between now and me taking the benefits?

Your pension plan may be invested in such a way that the value fluctuates on a daily basis. The underlying investments may for example be shares in companies that are quoted on a stock exchange. Investment market conditions will determine the value.

You may be quoted a value one day that is significantly lower within a matter of days. On the upside of course the value could be much higher at a later date.

You should treat any value that you are quoted by your pension plan provider as an indicative figure as it could be higher or lower when you actually start to take the benefits.

4. How do I prevent a fall in value?

If your pension plan is invested in a fund that can fall, or rise, in value you may be able to prevent this happening by switching funds.

Your pension plan provider may offer a cash, or guaranteed, fund into which you can switch your plan value. This will have the beneficial effect of providing you with some certainty.

There is a downside and that is you will miss out on any fund growth you might have received after you make the switch. You may consider it less stressful to have a certain value rather than missing out on prospective growth.

To carry out any switches you will usually have to give a written instruction to do this either by completing a switch form (supplied by the plan provider) or by writing a letter with your instructions. Some plan providers are prepared to do this over the phone.

5. Does my pension plan provide me with any guarantees (investment returns or guaranteed annuity rates)?

Some pension plans, particularly plans that were started before the late 1980s, may contain important guarantees.

It may be that the plan has a guaranteed annuity rate. Usually there is a table of guaranteed annuity rates depending upon your age at retirement. If you transfer your pension pot to another provider these guaranteed annuity rates will be lost.

As guaranteed annuity rates are typically much higher than those available today you should think very carefully before you transfer such a plan to a new provider.

You should note though that guaranteed annuity rates are typically very restricted. They may not for example make provision for a continued annuity income to a surviving spouse or partner.

These guarantees may also be quite restrictive on such things as the frequency of their timing, they may for example only be payable yearly. They may also not make any provision to protect the annuity income against inflation.

6. Do you provide any enhanced annuity benefits based on my medical history and smoker status?

As I mentioned earlier your pension plan provider probably does not know very much about you. They may not know, for example, that you are a smoker. They will be blissfully unaware that you have high blood pressure, diabetes, heart condition or suffer from a cancer.

Some pension plan providers have received criticism for not asking about their plan holder's state of health because such a medical condition can result in an enhanced retirement income if they choose to use their pension pot to purchase an annuity.

7. How much of the above value is available as a tax free cash lump sum?

The answer to this question is usually 25% of the value of the pension pot. There are some circumstances where the tax free cash amount is greater than 25% where the plan monies originated from an employer sponsored pension scheme where the tax free cash calculation method resulted in an enhanced amount of lump sum being available, but usually it is 25%.

It is worth checking just in case you can receive more of your pension pot as a tax free lump sum.

8. If I decide to take my benefits in a flexible fashion can you facilitate this?

From April 2015 it will be possible, if you wish to do so, to take the whole of your pension pot as a lump sum (flexi access).

The first 25% of the pension fund will be tax free. The balance of your pension pot will be subject to income tax at your marginal income tax rate.

In other words the taxable lump sum will be added to any other taxable income that you have to determine the rate of tax that you pay.

Some pension plan providers may be able to facilitate this option, others may not. You will need to ask your plan provider if they can do this and, importantly, if they will charge you to do this.

9. If I decide to move my plan value to another provider how quickly can you do this?

Dealing with some pension plan providers can be a long drawn out exercise. I have likened it to a war of attrition, where the winner is the one who persists.

I fully understand it is your money we are talking about, it is just that sometimes, it seems, the pension pot provider doesn't see it that way!

What should take a matter of a couple of days, a week tops, can sometimes take weeks or even months to complete. Plan ahead and start the process of accessing your pension pot benefits at least two months ahead of the date when you need to access your money.

10. As an existing client, will you give me any special terms if I keep my plan with you?

You would have thought that plan providers would be keen to keep their customers. Most businesses are willing to provide some added benefit to maintain the loyalty of their clients and facilitate repeat business.

It may be that your pension plan provider might offer a discount on plan charges if you take out a new plan with them. Many will not but if you don't ask you don't get!

Here are some things to consider once you have all the answers to the above questions. It may be that you have just one pension pot and have concluded that you can take your benefits from your current pension pot provider, in which case what follows isn't for you.

If you have a number of pension pots and you need to consider consolidating all those pots into one in order to make life easier then please do consider the following points before you decide to consolidate.

Your Existing Pension Pots

You may have one or more existing pension pots.

Typically, these pots will be have marketing titles such as Personal Pension Plans (PPPs) or Stakeholder Pension Plans (SHPs).

You may even have a Self-Invested Personal Pension (SIPP). This is one where you make more active decisions about the underlying plan investments.

You might also have a pension pot built up by virtue of being a member of an employer's occupational money purchase plan.

Fundamentally, these are all pretty much the same thing (a pot of money), but they may have different management charges that apply to them and you may have a range of investment fund choices.

Simply think of them as a number of pots of money that need to be gathered together so that you can start to spend the proceeds.

Tax free cash

One of the benefits that will be available to you is a Tax Free Cash lump sum and typically this will be worth 25% of the value of your plan.

In some instances the amount available to you may be greater than 25%.

This will be because the money in your pension pot originated from an employer sponsored occupational pension plan and was transferred to the personal pension plan when you left that employer.

If it is greater than 25% it will be because it benefited from protection in respect of benefits you built up in the original plan before April 2006 when the rules were different.

In the original scheme the calculation of the tax free cash was based on a formula (length of employment and earnings of the plan member) and this calculation basis might be carried over to the personal pension pot.

As an example, a client I helped recently was entitled to 32% of the plan value as a tax free cash lump sum.

Exit Charges

Your pension pot provider will tell you what your pension plan is currently worth. However, sometimes the value that you are quoted by them is not the same value that will be available to you if you transfer it to a new provider, the one who is going to pay you the benefits.

This transfer value difference may be down to plan charges that are applied to your pension pot or some adjustments made to the underlying investment fund (for example a market value adjustment to a with profits fund aimed at protecting those who remain in that fund rather than transfer out of it).

In other words if you transfer your money away from your pension pot provider to a new provider you will get less than the current value.

This sometimes occurs where you are taking benefits from the plan before the originally selected retirement age. For example, you may have a plan with a retirement age of 65 but have just attained age 63 when you want to start receiving benefits.

Such an early retirement or transfer penalty needs to be considered in light of its impact upon the value of your plan. If the penalty is very severe it may make more sense to defer taking the benefits until the penalty no longer applies or is more palatable.

Most of the time though there should be no exit penalty because you are taking the benefits at the same point in time as the originally selected retirement age or the plan has no exit penalties at any time.

Guaranteed Annuity Rates

Some older style pension pots contain an important benefit in the form of a guaranteed annuity rate (GAR).

A GAR means that you can usually convert your pot into an income level, with your existing provider, that is superior to anything available in the open market.

Often such GARs might be double the rate available in the open market, so to give up the GAR would be a very costly thing to do indeed. The higher the GAR the more income you would be giving up by transferring away.

Sometimes though these GARs are on a very specific basis, for example they make no provision for a surviving spouse's benefit or only allow income payments to be paid yearly.

However, the sensible thing to do is to check the policy conditions and see if you have such a guarantee in your pot.

Investment Choice

If you do *not* intend to buy an annuity with your pension pot but instead utilise Income drawdown and there is a sufficiently wide and suitable investment fund choice with your current pension pot provider you may decide not to move your money to a new provider at all.

Not all pension pot providers offer income drawdown in respect of your existing arrangements.

Cost

Cost is an important item to consider. There is little point in incurring new plan charges if they can be avoided and if your current plan is able to competitively provide the services that you require.

In many instances though, even if you stay with the original pension plan provider, they will require you to move your pension pot into a new arrangement, which facilitates Income drawdown or Flexi access benefits.

This is definitely where an Independent Financial Planner can assist.

They will do the analysis and research for you and ensure that you end up with the most suitable plan. Independent Financial Planners will consider the whole of market for plans that are suitable for you.

Do you need to move your pension funds?

If you don't need to move your plan then that will be good news. However, in very many instances there can be significant advantages in doing so.

The chances are there will be a provider who can offer a better annuity rate. Or a provider of a modern Income drawdown or Flexi access plan with better investment fund choice at lower cost and with much better information and service delivery.

Consolidating Your Pension Pots

If you have a number of pension pots and decide that you want to bring them altogether ahead of taking retirement benefits I would refer to this action as "consolidation". This can be done before or at the time you decide to take the benefits.

Where you either want to take just your entitlement to the tax free cash lump sum, or fully utilise Income drawdown or Flexi access, then you will usually consolidate your various plans. This will make managing the remaining investment funds simpler.

Consolidation makes it easier to manage your pension pot investments and certainly easier to predict and project the benefits that might emerge from your pot. By moving to a modern arrangement you can also exercise a much greater degree of control over your money.

For example you might choose a modern pension pot where all of the pension investments are visible to you on a computer screen. Sometimes these are referred to as platforms.

These modern arrangements make life much easier for you, they are often cheaper than conventional pension arrangements provided by insurance companies and usually offer a very wide range of investment fund choice.

They are generally also cost effective ways of managing your pension pot, buying and selling the underlying investment funds at low cost, with or without the services of a financial adviser.

About Your Pension Pot – The Questions

Once again, you may not yet have all the answers about your pension pot so to make life easier for you here they are again without my commentary.

1. What is the current value of my pension plan?

2. Is this valuable available to me if I decide to take the benefits now either from you or from another provider?

3. Can the quoted value of my pension plan fall between now and me taking the benefits?

4. How do I prevent a fall in value?

5. Does my pension plan provide me with any guarantees (investment returns or guaranteed annuity rates)?

6. Do you provide any enhanced annuity benefits based on my medical history and smoker status?

7. How much of the above value is available as a tax free cash lump sum?

8. If I decide to take my benefits in a flexible fashion can you facilitate this?

9. If I decide to move my plan value to another provider how quickly can you do this?

10. As an existing client will you give me special terms if I keep my plan with you?

Chapter Four
Your Choices and Options

Your Choices and Options

In essence you will have at least the following six choices in respect of your pension pot;

- **Deferral**–You can defer doing anything at all and wait until some date in the future to take your benefits;

- **Tax free cash**–You can choose to take your entitlement to the tax free cash lump sum and no other benefits;

- **Annuity**–You can choose to use your pension pot to buy an annuity - including specialist annuity products (having first of all taken any entitlement to the tax free cash lump sum if you wish to do so);

- **Income drawdown**–You can use your pension pot in an "income drawdown" arrangement (having first taken any entitlement to a tax free cash lump sum if you wish to do so).

- **Flexi-access**–You can take the whole of your pension fund as a lump sum, the first 25% as a tax free cash lump sum and the balance of the pension pot subject to income tax (from April 2015 in most cases).

- **Mix and match**–You can of course mix and match the above and combine the benefits of each approach.

Which of these choices is going to be the most suitable for you? The answer is of course "it depends".

It depends upon so many things and that is why you need to think carefully before you make a decision.

In this chapter I have described the main options and as well as asking you lots of questions I have also described some circumstances where the option seems to be the best one available.

Remember each approach has both advantages and disadvantages and they need to be carefully considered.

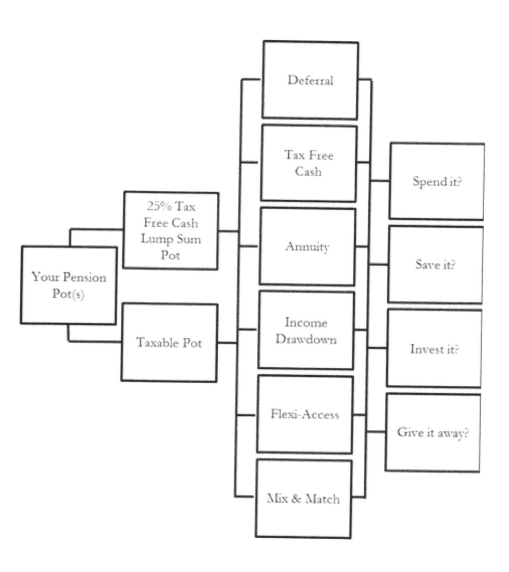

Deferral–You can defer doing anything at all and wait until some date in the future to take your benefits;

You do not have to take any benefits from your pension pot even at the selected retirement date shown on your policy documents. You may have told your pension pot provider, when you set up your plan, that you would retire at age 60 say. There is nothing to prevent you deferring taking your benefits.

You may decide that you want to carry on working for a further five years and wait to take your benefits at that time.

You may be thinking of your pension pot as sum of money that you want to pass onto the next generation when you die.

You may decide to defer taking any benefits so that in the event of your death that pot of money can be received by children or grandchildren for them to enjoy. Alternatively you may want your spouse or partner to benefit from your pension fund capital.

Even if you don't carry on working you may have income from other sources, savings and investments, that you can use to fund your income needs in a more tax efficient fashion than the taxable income that you could receive from your pension pot.

There are advantages and disadvantages as a result of deferral and these are shown below.

Advantages

- You effectively defer making the decisions. Well most of them, because you may still need to decide how your pension pot is invested between now and taking the benefits;

- You may be able to enjoy better benefits in the future by virtue of the value of your pension pot rising and possibly better future annuity rates;

- In the event of your death the value of the pension pot can usually be passed onto your family tax free;

Disadvantages

- You don't get to enjoy the benefits now. You have worked and saved hard to build your pension pot and you might miss out on spending that money if you were, for example, to die before you took the benefits;

- There is no guarantee that the benefits will be higher in the future. The value of the investments in your pension pot can go down as well as up;

- It may need a lot of investment growth in order to make up for each year's worth of income that you have not taken.

Tax free cash–You can choose to take your entitlement to the tax free cash lump sum and no other benefits;

One of the benefits that will be available to you is a Tax Free Cash lump sum and typically this will be worth 25% of the value of your plan.

More than 25%

In some instances the amount available may be greater than 25% (as described on page 40).

Advantages

- You get to enjoy the money now and you can do with it whatever you want;

- There is no tax to pay (that's why it is called a tax free cash lump sum);

- You don't have to take any taxable income;

- You can leave the rest of your pension pot invested for the future.

- If you take tax free cash now it can help to set an investment target for example to make your pension pot grow back to its current value over x years.

Disadvantages

- Taking tax free cash now might reduce your future level of retirement benefits;

- You may have to move your existing pension pot to a new plan or new provider (or both) to facilitate the taking of the tax free cash lump sum;

- You will still have to pay management charges for the future investment management of the balance of your pension pot;

- The amount of tax free cash that your pension pot might have provided in the future might have been higher than the current amount you have taken.

Annuity–You can choose to use your pension pot to buy an annuity— including specialist annuity products (having first of all taken any entitlement to the tax free cash lump sum if you wish to do so);

The most common method of converting a pension fund into income is by using your pension fund to purchase an **Annuity.**

For many people this is becoming a less attractive option because annuity rates are currently quite low and some people challenge whether they will ever get value for money from such an arrangement.

What is an annuity?

Put simply, it is a financial instrument for converting capital into income.

You hand over the income producing part of your pension fund to an annuity provider (An insurance company) and in return they promise to pay you an income for the rest of your life.

How is the amount of your annuity income calculated?

The annuity rate is made up of a number of factors. The first factor is your age, because this will determine your anticipated life expectancy and thus for how long the annuity provider is likely to have to pay out the income benefits.

The annuity rate will also be determined by reference to the yields on long-term investment assets typically Government Bonds or Gilts, Corporate Bonds and other investment assets. This is because the annuity payment to you is a liability to the insurance company. The Government requires that the annuity provider match their liabilities to such assets.

Part of the annuity rate will also be made up of the expenses incurred by the annuity provider in marketing their product and also an element of profit for them.

There are other factors that will determine the actual rate and amount of annuity that you might receive and we have detailed those below.

Conventional Annuity

By conventional I mean an annuity that does not have any element of investment risk associated with it.

It is simply a contract where you exchange the capital value of your pension pot in return for which the insurance company will pay you a gross annual income for the rest of your life (and possibly the rest of the life of a survivor).

One of the unattractive features of an annuity is that the pension pot owner often feels that he has handed over a significant amount of capital to the annuity provider and that he will not live long enough to have received the whole value of his pension pot back from them.

In some instances this will be true of course, because if the annuitant dies too soon then the balance of the pension pot will be kept by the annuity provider.

There is no getting away from the fact that annuity business represents a highly profitable business stream for the insurance company that markets them. However the changes that have been introduced will probably see, at least in the short term a reduction in demand for annuity products.

The annuity providers might though respond to this challenge by introducing a more flexible range of annuity products.

Longevity

In my experience people tend to considerably underestimate their life expectancy. Consider the consequences of outliving the actuarial tables.

If you purchased your annuity at age 60 and lived to be 95 then those 35 years would see the gross annual annuity paid out each and every year.

At an assumed annuity rate of 5.5% that means that 192.5% of the value of the pension plan will have been paid out. Even if the annuitant *only* lived to 85 years old 137.5% of the value of the pension plan pot will have been paid out in annual annuity instalments.

But the value argument is not just about the total income received it is also about the fact that the annuity provider will have received the capital value of the pension pot. Surely, they could have invested that capital and achieved an income yield of 5.5%?

This argument seems quite reasonable but we all know that in seeking to achieve a yield of 5.5% the pension pot would need to be invested in a risk environment.

Consider that even a multi-asset class fund for a cautious investor runs the risk of seeing the value fall in some years and sometimes fall quite sharply.

So think of an annuity as a trade-off between the value of your pension pot and the certainty of gross income, paid to you for as long as you live. In essence it is a kind of insurance policy against living too long, or at least an insurance policy against outliving your pension pot!

An alternative to purchasing an annuity is to consider income drawdown and that alternative carries both investment risk and future interest rate risk (although the so-called 'Third Way' alternative of combining temporary annuities and income drawdown is also worth considering).

Investment Linked Annuity

Unlike a conventional annuity an investment linked annuity provides the opportunity for increasing future income based on investment returns. In selecting such an annuity your income will be linked to the performance of an investment fund or funds.

I am sure that you will realise that if the level of annuity income from an investment linked annuity can rise, based on investment fund performance, then it can also fall in value if performance is less good. So the future level of annuity income from an investment linked annuity is not usually guaranteed.

With investment linked annuities you are typically required to establish a starting level of annuity income based on future anticipated investment returns. The more optimistic the expected investment returns the higher the starting level of the annuity income.

Watch out though because if these returns are not achieved there could be a substantial fall in the future income level.

Some annuitants like the thought of an investment linked income but find the volatility associated with investment funds just a little too rich for their taste. They therefore choose a with-profits annuity where the investment peaks and troughs are smoothed over time.

When investment returns are good, with profits bonuses are added to the annuity value. Again these are not without risk plans but considered by some to be potentially less risky.

Sorry to be repetitive, but the emphasis here is that investment linked annuities are not without risk.

Impaired Life Annuity

An annuity rate reflects the expected life expectancy of the annuitant. So what if that life expectancy is reduced due to some pre-existing medical condition or medical history? Or what if the annuitant has a lifestyle that might result in a reduced life expectancy (for example smoking)?

Well, not unexpectedly, they might be able to secure a higher annuity rate than someone who is an average or standard risk.

Such enhanced annuities are called impaired life annuities and are very attractive to the pension pot owner who seeks the benefit of a guaranteed stream of gross income but feels that they are not going to live as long as someone without their medical condition or lifestyle.

The impaired life annuity is subject to an underwriting process where a medical application form is completed and where the underwriter for the annuity provider may ask for further medial information (from the annuitant's GP for example) in order to demonstrate the existence of a medical condition or history that might shorten the annuitant's life.

The impaired life annuity can therefore offer a significantly higher level of annuity income than a standard annuity.

Be careful if you take the annuity income on offer from the provider of your current pension pot because they will probably not have taken into account your medical history or your smoker status if you are, and you may be missing out on the higher income available from an impaired life annuity.

Single Life Annuity

The annuity is based on your life and if you are single (no spouse or civil partner) then that is probably perfectly satisfactory for you.

A single life annuity income is higher than one for a person of the same age which incorporates a survivor's pension.

However, there are some circumstances where even a married person might choose a higher single life annuity, perhaps where there are other significant financial assets available to take care of any survivor.

Joint Life Annuity

If you are married or have a partner then you will need to think about whether you want your annuity income to be paid to that person in the event of your death.

You can arrange a joint life annuity and the payments will be a lower amount than a single life annuity but of course will continue to be paid, at 100%, 67% or 50% of the annuity level, to your spouse or partner as long as they do not pre-decease you.

Level Annuity

You can choose an annuity that remains at the same level for as long as you live. This is the highest starting amount for an annuity and many people buy their annuity on this basis because they underestimate the damage that future inflation can do to their fixed income.

Or, they simply do not believe they are going to live long enough for an increasing annuity, which starts at a lower level, to provide value for money.

Escalating

An escalating annuity increases each year that it is paid to you. You choose the rate at which the annuity income increases (see below).

As it will increase each year, in the first year it will start at a lower amount than a level annuity. How much lower will depend upon the type of escalation selected.

Fixed Percentage

You may choose a fixed rate of escalation, for example 3%. If future inflation rates exceed 3% the purchasing power of your annuity income will be reduced.

If future inflation rates are lower than 3% then the opposite will apply and the purchasing power of your annuity income will be greater in the future.

RPI

You may ask that your annuity income increases in line with inflation (as measured by the Retail Prices Index or RPI).

If you do this then you need not worry about inflation eroding the purchasing power of your annuity in the future *but* the starting amount of your annuity will be much lower than the starting amount of a level annuity.

It will take many years (12 years or so depending upon the rate of inflation) for your RPI linked annuity to rise to the same amount as a level annuity. It will then take a number of further years before you have enjoyed as much net income.

However, if you live long enough, or if inflation is at a significant rate, an RPI linked annuity will be really good value for money.

Guarantees

What if you die too soon? The annuity income will of course be payable for as long as you live. So the guarantee periods described below only apply in the early years of the annuity payments.

5 years

Imagine that you buy your annuity today and then die after 3 years. The 5 year guarantee means that 2 further years' worth of the annuity will become payable to your beneficiaries.

Usually this will be paid as a lump sum. Assuming you have a single life annuity, then payments will stop at that point. If you have a joint life annuity and your spouse or partner is still alive, annuity income will continue, after the guaranteed period, to be paid to them.

10 years

You may not feel that 5 years is a long enough guaranteed period and may prefer a longer period, for example 10 years.

The starting amount of the annuity will be lower for a 10 year guarantee than it is for a 5 year guarantee and of course both will be lower than for an annuity which has no early death guarantee. But of course if you die too soon, more will be paid to your estate.

Value protection

If you really are put off an annuity because you don't want the annuity provider to keep the balance of your pension pot in the event that you die too soon, you may be able to arrange an annuity where the balance of your pension pot, less the annuity instalments you have received is returned on your death. The starting point for such an annuity will be lower than one without this protection.

Frequency

If you are working you probably receive your salary on a monthly basis. You may feel that post retirement it is most convenient to continue to receive pension annuity payments at the same frequency as your income was paid.

This will enable you to work out your financial budget. But you can choose a different frequency if you wish, for example quarterly or half-yearly or even just yearly.

In Advance or In Arrears

If you receive the first annuity instalment as soon as you hand your pension fund over to the annuity provider then such payments are said to be paid in advance.

If you defer the payments, say until the end of the next month, (or quarter or half-year or year) then such payments are said to be paid in arrears. In advance payments are lower than in arrear payments.

What type of annuity is right for you?

As a starting point consider the following questions and make sure you understand the reasons for the general considerations.

Are you married or have a partner? If yes, consider a joint life annuity.

Do you have a medical condition or a medical history that might reduce your life expectancy? If yes, consider an impaired life annuity.

Are you or your spouse or partner a smoker? If yes, consider an impaired life annuity.

If you die too soon, do you want a minimum guaranteed income payment? If yes, consider a 5 or 10 year guarantee.

Do you want the highest level of starting annuity income? If yes, consider a level annuity.

Are you concerned about future price inflation? If yes, consider an escalating annuity.

Are you prepared to take on a degree of investment risk to achieve a higher future income? If yes, consider an investment linked annuity.

Income drawdown–You can use your pension pot in an income drawdown arrangement (having first taken any entitlement to a tax free cash lump sum if you wish to do so).

Income drawdown is where the pension fund remains invested and income is drawn from it. This is not without risk and cost and is not right for everyone, even those disappointed by low annuity rates.

There are a number of reasons why you might consider an income drawdown arrangement rather than purchasing an annuity with your pension plan fund. You may feel that in the future annuity rates might be superior to those available today.

Typically, because you will be older in the future (stating the obvious I know!) annuity rates might be expected to be higher, but there is no guarantee of this.

One prime reason for choosing income drawdown over say, an annuity, is that in the event of death the balance of the income drawdown fund can be available as a lump sum that might be passed on to the next generation.

This will rarely be the case with an annuity (apart from, for example, payments in respect of guaranteed periods).

The term income drawdown currently still applies even if you have decided just to take your entitlement to the tax free cash lump sum and *no income*.

Investment Risk

I want to over emphasise the word risk in this book, but I feel that is a healthy thing to do, because it is the case that income drawdown is not without risk.

For this type of pension pot to work well you are going to have to continue to invest your pension monies. Remember, the value of investments can fall as well as rise and you may not get back as much as you invest.

You will want to make your Income drawdown fund grow for a number of reasons;

- You will want to replace the income that you have drawn from it;

- You will want to cover any plan charges that are applicable;

- You will want to try to keep pace with future inflation rates; and

- You will want to recognise that you are missing out on "mortality gain" by not buying an annuity now (see below).

(Mortality gain is recognition that part of an annuity rate (that you didn't buy) is made up of the fact that some people who buy an annuity die too soon and the annuity provider effectively pays some of their savings to annuitants who continue to live.

If you choose the income drawdown route you simply miss out on that mortality gain and your pension fund will need to grow in value to replace it. I know it sounds a bit morbid but it is important to note.

So your income drawdown fund needs to grow for a whole host of reasons and frankly it isn't going to do this if you take the safe option and keep it all in cash.

You are going to have to actively invest it and accept that the value of your plan (and indeed the income from it) will fluctuate over time.

Extraction of Income

You can decide the frequency of the rate of withdrawal of the income from your pot . Most people take a monthly payment just like they would have done whilst they were working and just like most pension payments that they might receive.

You can choose instead though to take less regular payments, for example yearly, and chop and change this over time. In fact, you can change the frequency of payments as often as you like.

In the context of investing your income drawdown pot where should income payments come from? I would recommend that they come from a cash fund.

I appreciate I said earlier that you should invest your income drawdown pot, but some of it should be held in cash to pay plan charges and from which income payments should be extracted.

This means then that you will not have to disinvest from assets such as shares, at an inappropriate time, perhaps when share prices have fallen.

As a general rule of thumb I believe that two to three years of income might be held as cash and then over time this cash can be replaced by profits from more volatile investments.

I hope that the following six step process helps explain how income drawdown pots should be invested.

Six Step Investment Process

You should follow a robust investment process because experience tells us this is where the best outcomes are likely to emerge.

Step one

Always make investment decisions that are linked to your goals and objectives. When do you intend to take benefits?

The shorter the term until that point in time, the more cautious you might be about the degree of investment risk that you need to take.

How much income do you need your pension fund to generate to enable you to have the retirement lifestyle you want?

Take into account any other investment assets that might generate retirement income for you as well as any other sources of retirement income (for example the State Pension). How hard does your pension pot have to work? This will dictate the degree of risk that you may need to take with your pot.

Step two

Establish your attitude towards investment risk, reward and volatility and your capacity for investment loss.

Step three

Once you have established a risk profile for yourself the next step will be to create an investment asset class model that matches your appetite for risk and your capacity for loss.

Essentially this means deciding the percentage of your pension pot that will be held in different asset classes. How much will you keep in cash, fixed-interest securities (bonds) commercial property and equities (shares in UK and International companies)?

Remember the old adage about "not keeping all your eggs in one basket?" This is what asset class modelling seeks to do.

Whilst it does not always work out this way, it is generally the case that when some investment asset class values are rising (say shares) others are falling (say bonds).

Asset class modelling seeks to reduce the worst of the investment downside rather than chasing double digit returns and trying to shoot the lights out!

In our experience most people are more comfortable with lower risk with their pension pots than an aggressive or speculative approach.

Step four

Just because we have created an investment asset class model at the start of the investment of your income drawdown pot it does not mean that we cannot change it in the future.

As economic and investment market conditions change it makes perfect sense to rebalance and alter the original model.

We are not advocating trying to time the market but modest movements between the investment asset classes over time does make real sense particularly where it is to reduce the overall risk profile of the portfolio, perhaps by taking the steps of moving a little from equities to cash and bonds for example.

Step five

Now you can select the underlying investment funds to marry up to the investment asset class model.

You can do this by selecting single asset class funds for yourself, ask a financial adviser to help you do this or you can outsource this to a fund manager and buy a multi-asset class fund where the fund manager selects the mix.

Step six

The worst investment decisions in our experience are the ones that are made and then never reviewed. You should ensure that you have an investment review process in place.

At least once a year take the time to review your pension pot and challenge the performance of the funds.

Make sure that the funds continue to remain suitable for you bearing in mind your financial planning goals and objectives and your tolerance and appetite for risk. An annual review is also a good time to rebalance your pension pot investment portfolio in line with your risk profile.

Flexi-access (from 6 April 2015) You can take advantage of the freedom and choice in pension's options and take the whole of your pension fund all in one go if you wish.

You can effectively treat your pension pot as if it were a bank account and withdraw sums to fund your retirement lifestyle. Some of those funds can be taken tax free and some are subject to income tax.

At this point in time providers of such arrangements are playing their cards close to their chests with an absence of detail such as how much they will charge to facilitate such a service.

Providers of pensions, in the main, are not used to pot owners dipping in and out of their pension pots as when they feel they want to.

Income drawdown is a much more structured approach to taking benefits from a pension pot and the providers have never been shy about charging the pot owner for withdrawals. It will therefore be interesting to see the charging structures as they emerge.

Small pots

For some years it has been possible for owners of small pension pots to take the entirety of their benefits in the form of a lump sum.

The first 25% of the pot is tax free and the balance subject to income tax. What Flexi-access plans do is to extend this facility to everyone regardless of the size of the pot

Advantages

- Complete freedom of choice about what you do with your pension pot. Spend it, save it, invest it or give it away;

- No need to hand it over to an annuity provider (although to be fair that has been the case for many years);

- Putting you in control. If you need your pension pot monies to provide income for the rest of your life it will be down to you to decide the pace at which you spend it and what you do with the money in the meantime is entirely up to you.

- Tax planning. If you take the pension pot monies and you have no other taxable income you might be able to arrange withdrawals in such a way that they do not exceed your annual personal tax allowance. You could effectively take the benefits tax free over a number of years.

- Taking the benefits might allow you to enjoy early retirement. If you are due to receive state pension benefits and other pension benefits in a few years' time imagine being able to quit your job and spend your pension pot to fund early retirement?

- You don't have to take all of the money from your pension pot in one go. You could phase this in over time not just to avoid paying large amounts of income tax but to ensure you have sufficient money later on in life.

Disadvantages

- The balance of your pension pot (after the first 25%) is subject to income tax. If you take the whole of your pension pot in one lump sum you may have to pay a substantial amount of income tax at 20%, 40% or even 45%.

- None of us knows how long we are going to live. If we spend our pension pot too quickly we may not have enough money later on in life to live the retirement life we want to live.

- If you take all of your pension pot as a lump sum you may still have to decide what to do with that money. You may have to continue to make investment or savings decisions. The place where you invest or save your pension pot monies may not be as tax privileged as the pension pot from which you took the money.

Mix & Match You can use all of the above choices and blend together the methods of taking money from your pension pot in a way that best suits your needs and wants.

Phasing in of benefits over time and using a combination of the different approaches to managing your pension pot might make real sense.

Advantages

- You may want to defer making the decision about buying an annuity in the hope that the annuity rates improve in the future. Alternatively you might want to use some of your pension pot to buy an annuity to secure a guaranteed income to pay the essential household bills;

- If your state of health deteriorates in the future you may become entitled to an impaired life annuity and by not buying an annuity now you may get a higher future income;

- You might decide to keep some of your pension pot invested for the future in the expectation that you will have a larger pension pot with which to fund your retirement;

- You might use mixing & matching to fund immediate/early retirement with a view to receiving other income (state pension, occupational pensions) at a later date;

- You might want to take some or all of your tax free cash lump sum now and defer taking any taxable benefits until a later date. I have experienced some clients successfully spending their tax free cash lump sum as if it were income over a number of years and only taking taxable benefits from their pension pot at a later date.

- Pension pot benefits not taken will still constitute important benefits on your death for your family

Disadvantages

- If you don't take all the benefits now you may not live long enough to "enjoy" them in the future, none of us knows how long we are going to live;

- If you keep some of your pension pot invested you will have to continue to make investment decisions and there will be management costs incurred in the future;

There is no guarantee of course that by deferring taking benefits in whole or in part now, that you will be better off financially in the future.

Chapter Five
Case Studies

Case Studies

Deferral

Patrick and Charlotte have decided to retire. Charlotte is in receipt of her state pension and a small NHS pension benefit. Patrick has received a statement from his ex-employer's pension scheme describing his entitlement to a tax free cash lump sum and pension income.

If Patrick takes his entitlement to the maximum tax free cash lump sum from his ex-employer's scheme then in the event of his death, Charlotte will continue to receive 2/3rds of the pension that is payable to Patrick.

They have completed a retirement budget and have concluded that the pension income that they receive from all sources is sufficient for their needs over the next few years. During his working lifetime Patrick has acquired three pension pots (in addition to his employer's pension scheme). His main concern is that in the event of his death Charlotte will be provided for financially.

Patrick has been considering buying an annuity with a 100% survivor's payment to Charlotte. He is not however impressed by the current annuity rates on offer.

The tax free cash lump sum from his employer's pension scheme together with other cash savings and investments they have means that they don't need to take any further tax free cash from Patrick's pension pots (although they may do that in the future as they want to help their two sons buy homes for their young families).

Patrick decides to defer taking any benefits from his pension pots at the present time. In the event of Patrick's death before age 75 the pension pot can be paid to Charlotte or their children without any tax liability.

He will of course need to make sure that the pension pots are invested in line with his appetite for investment risk and reward.

Tax free cash

Fiona is 57 years old. She is self-employed, loves what she does and really has no intention of retiring anytime soon.

Over the years Fiona has been very prudent and saved in a pension pot. She sees this as a safety net and if she was unable to work in the future, perhaps because ill-health prevented it, she might then draw upon her pension pot.

Her son, Andrew, has finished University and has decided that he wants to start his own business. Fiona is keen to help him she believes that he has a good business concept and that it is likely to succeed.

Rather than going to the bank to raise finance Fiona has agreed to take some of her entitlement to tax free cash from her pension pot and lend it to Andrew. He has agreed to repay the loan by monthly instalments. Being the generous Mother that she is, Fiona has agreed the loan will be interest free.

Fiona can take part of her entitlement to a tax free cash lump sum without taking any immediate pension income. If she needs to, she can take further tax free cash in the future.

Annuity

Robin is very risk averse. He has never taken much investment risk during his working life and has decided that what is most important to him is absolute certainty of income during his retirement years.

He has plans to travel and enjoy his interests with his friends.

Robin suffers from high blood pressure for which he takes medication and three years ago suffered a heart attack. He has recovered well from that event. It does mean though that he is entitled to apply for an impaired life annuity. He is able to obtain an annuity about 35% higher than the standard available rate.

After taking his tax free cash lump sum he uses the balance of his pension pot to buy an annuity from a specialist annuity provider. As Robin has no spouse/partner and no one else that he wants to provide for on his death he chooses a single life annuity payable to him each month.

Just in case he dies too soon, Robin has arranged his annuity with a five year guarantee (so that if he dies in the first five years after starting the annuity the balance of those five years payments will form part of his estate- his friends are the beneficiaries in his will).

Robin considers the difference between a level annuity and one that increases over time to help protect against inflation, but he chooses the higher starting amount of the level annuity. He expects to protect himself against future inflation by spending his savings.

Robin enjoys the certainty that the annuity income will be payable for as long as he lives.

Income drawdown

Ben does not like the thought of handing over a significant sum of money to an annuity provider.

Not only does he think that current annuity rates represent poor value he believes that he can invest his pension pot in such a way that he can get a better income than he would from an annuity and still pass on money to his children and grandchildren.

Ben chooses an income drawdown plan. The maximum income that he can take from his pension pot is capped by government rules at about 150% of the level of an annuity that might have been payable to him Ben has to consider a number of important things to make income drawdown work;

- He needs to make sure that he doesn't erode his pension pot too quickly by taking too much income (particularly during periods when investment market conditions and returns are poor);

- He needs to invest his pension fund in a range of investment assets. Sensibly, Ben puts enough of his pension pot into cash to use for his first two to three years of income withdrawal, this means he won't have to cash in investments in the short term if investment market conditions go against him;

- Like everyone with a pension pot Ben needs to consider his life expectancy and how long his pension pot is going to have to work for him.

Flexi access

Julia has a pension pot of £43,000. She will start to receive her state pension in four years' time. For some time she has been hearing from her pension pot provider that she can take 25% of her pension pot as a tax free cash lump sum and that the remainder of her fund must be used to provide retirement income.

Her pension pot provider tells her that "the most common way to do this is to use your fund to buy an annuity." Julia is adamant that she doesn't want to do this.

Instead she has a plan; she will take her tax free cash lump sum (£10,750) and spend that over the next year as income as Julia has always been a basic rate tax payer she recognises that this is equivalent to taxed income of £13,438 per year or £1,119 per month, enough for her to live on.

Next year she will take a further £10,600 from her pension pot. As this is equivalent to her personal tax allowance she will again have no tax to pay. She can then do this for the next two years.

Effectively she can take the whole of her pension fund, if she chooses to do so, income tax free.

Julia wants to do this because she does not enjoy her job at all. She has worked out that it means she can stop or reduce the amount of work she does now, rather than continuing to work full- time for the next four years.

Mix & Match

Mike & Nicola are pretty uncertain about the future. Now that the children have flown the nest they are seriously considering some changes in their lives.

For some time they have both been pretty fed up with their jobs. There is a good possibility that they will downsize their home and buy a smaller place away from the City.

They are also considering buying a place in France.

Nicola is 14 years younger than Mike and whilst they might want some certainty of income Mike has worked out that a single life annuity might be better value than one which provides a survivor's pension for Nicola. He may use enough of his pension pot to buy an annuity that covers off their important bills each month.

They will probably not need to take tax free cash from Mike's pension pot as selling their home is going to free up a lot of capital even after they have purchased replacement property in the UK and France.

Mike thinks he should defer taking the bulk of his pension pot money until they have finalised their plans.

Nicola likes the changes to the pension pot rules. She will definitely consider the Flexi access approach and take money from her pension pot and she will probably combine tax free cash payments and taxable lump sums in order to ensure she doesn't have to pay too much income tax.

Chapter Six
About Guidance and Advice

About Guidance and Advice

When you decide to take the benefits from your pension pot there are three approaches you might choose to adopt.

DIY

You might choose to do it yourself.

You can gather the information you need about your pension pot (you might use the questions we posed earlier).

Your pension plan provider will send to you the wake-up pack with the information that they think you need. You can then work out what is best for you and implement your plan of action.

You don't always need an adviser to do this for you. You can arrange any replacement pension product that you might need online.

However, you need to consider that some of the choices that are available to you, if you implement them, are irrevocable. An annuity purchase for example is literally for life. Get the wrong type of annuity now and you will definitely get the chance to repent at leisure.

Guidance

You might go for the guidance service that has been put in place by Government and paid for by a levy on the financial services sector.

If you do you can have a telephone conversation with a representative from The Pensions Advisory Service (TPAS) www.pensionsadvisoryservice.org. uk or a face-face meeting with a representative from the Citizens Advice Bureau (CAB) www.citizensadvice.org.uk.

Advice

TPAS or CAB are unable able to provide you with "advice" (I know, they have the word Advice in their title) but there is a lot of difference between "guidance" and "advice" delivered by an authorised and regulated financial adviser, as you will see from the following table.

You might go to www.unbiased.co.uk to find a shortlist of local independent financial advisers.

You can get an enormous amount of information and guidance from the Internet. But remember, the Internet is both a brilliant source of information and also dis-information! Be careful how you use it.

Guidance vs. Advice

Whilst some people use these two words interchangeably in the context of your pension pot they are very different creatures indeed. I have set out below a comparison between the two to help you decide which you think you need.

There is the possibility that you will seek the free guidance service and then realise that you need to pay for professional advice but hopefully you will still learn a lot about your choices and options along the way.

	Guidance	Advice
Will I receive specific advice and recommendations about what I should do?	No. Guidance is not Advice. It can help you to "think" about what you might do but it cannot replace specific advice and recommendations as to what you "should" do.	Yes. Your adviser will provide specific advice and recommendations and tell you exactly what you should do
Will I be told about the advantages and disadvantages of any course of action?	Yes. There are advantages and disadvantages to any course of action with your pension plan and the guidance service should highlight these.	Yes. Your adviser will describe the advantages and disadvantages of any course of action that they recommend and will place equal emphasis on them.
Will the guidance provider or adviser obtain detailed information about my existing pension arrangements for me?	No. The guidance provider will ask you a lot of questions to help you think about your choices and options but you will have to provide them with details about your existing retirement pots provided by your plan provider.	Yes. Your adviser will ask you to provide a letter(s) of authority and will then do this work for you. They will obtain detailed information about your existing retirement pots from each of your plan providers.
Will the guidance service provider or the adviser be covered by Professional Indemnity Insurance and be subject to the Financial Ombudsman Service (FOS) rulings if a complaint is made and also protected by the Financial Services Compensation Scheme (FSCS)?	No. Remember this is not authorised and regulated advice and the guidance service provider is not therefore required to offer these protections.	Yes. Your adviser will provide authorised and regulated advice and will therefore be required to offer these important protections.

	Guidance	Advice
Will the guidance service provider or adviser provide me with a written report detailing the actions I need to take?	Yes. The guidance service provider will confirm back to you the sorts of things that you need to think about before you make any decisions.	Yes. Your adviser will confirm their advice and recommendations in writing before you proceed. This will typically be in the form of a detailed report or a suitability letter. Your adviser will discuss this report/letter with you so that you have the chance to ask and have answered any questions that arise.
Will I receive specific, personalised illustrations of the pension product solutions being recommended?	No. You will not receive a specific recommendation and the service provider will not therefore present you with specific personalised illustrations.	Yes. Your adviser will present to you personalised and specific illustrations of any plan recommendations that they make. They will describe costs and charges and risk associated with their recommendations.
Will I be told which product provider I should use to provide my retirement benefits?	No. Remember it is guidance and not advice.	Yes. Your adviser will research the whole of market and select plans that they believe based on their professional judgement are best for you.
Will I have to pay anything to the guidance service provider or adviser?	No. the cost of the guidance will be borne by a levy on the financial services industry including the adviser community.	Yes. Your adviser will charge you for their professional services. Their charge will be disclosed to you in advance of any work commencing.

	Guidance	Advice
What is "signposting" and what value does it provide to me?	Your pension provider will signpost you (point you to) the guidance service available from The Pensions Advisory Service (TPAS) or Citizens advice Bureaux (CAB). If TPAS or CAB believe you should seek advice they will signpost (point you to) advisors- you probably thought about doing that anyway!	Advisers don't "sign post" they give specific advice and recommendations- this is much more valuable than signposting.
Will the guidance service provider or adviser remove the "stress" of making "at retirement" choices?	If you wanted to know exactly what to do with your pension pot, not really, no.	Yes. Your adviser will de-stress the at retirement making decisions.

If you decide to employ a professional adviser to help you decide what best to do with your pension pot here are some good questions to ask them;

1. Do you provide independent, impartial advice?

There are two distinct types of authorised and regulated financial advisers. There are independent financial advisers and there are restricted advisers.

The former are required by their regulator (the Financial Conduct Authority or FCA) to demonstrate their independence by examining all the suitable products available to you to convert your pension pot into retirement benefits.

Restricted advisers do not have to consider all the alternatives for you but can restrict their advice to a more limited range of choices and options.

If you engage with a financial adviser they must tell you, ahead of doing any chargeable work for you, what their status is, whether they are independent or restricted.

In my view (and I would say this wouldn't I?) the choices and options that you have at retirement are so wide ranging and complex, and the product solutions available to you so variable, that you should take independent financial advice.

2. What experience do you have in providing at retirement advice?

Experience is vital in selecting the right adviser for you. Here I am not thinking so much about duration, 5, 10 or 15 years, but hands on experience in dealing with multiple clients with different goals and objectives.

Ask the adviser to talk you through some client scenarios and how they approached the advice that they provided to their client. A competent adviser will be able to describe to you the sort of questions that they will use to establish how they are going to determine what is right for you.

3. What qualifications do you have in providing at retirement advice?

Like experience, qualifications on their own are not a good determining factor in choosing an adviser. Qualifications and experience are not mutually exclusive though and a good mix of the two is probably worth looking for.

To provide advice to a UK consumer an authorised and regulated adviser needs to have passed certain examinations and on a national level those are known as QCF level 4. They are Diploma level qualifications.

Many advisers have chosen to qualify to a much higher standard QCF level 6 and have Chartered Financial Planner or Certified Financial Planner (CFP) status. I believe that the complexities of at retirement choices are such that a QCF Level 6 adviser is most appropriate to help you.

All authorised and regulated advisers must hold a Statement of Professional Standing (SPS) demonstrating that they have the required qualifications and are members of a professional body whose code of conduct and ethics they have signed up to.

So, in summary, look for a suitable qualified, experienced and ethical adviser to help you with your at retirement choices and options. Asking a friend, relative or work colleague for a recommendation is probably a good starting point in your selection process.

4. Can you provide me with any references from existing at retirement clients?

A suitably experienced and qualified adviser will be delighted to provide you with references from their clients. After all what a compliment it is to receive a reference from a satisfied client?

Reluctance on the part of the adviser to provide a reference for you or indeed a reluctance upon clients to provide such references for their adviser should be a signal worth noting!

5. What are your charges? (Initial fees and on-going service fees)

In the same way that advisers have to disclose their status before doing any work for their clients they also have to disclose their charges before completing any chargeable activity.

Transparency is the key here. Even if the adviser charges a fee based on a percentage of the amount that the client has to invest they have to convert that percentage charge into an indicative monetary amount.

There are generally three chargeable steps in the advice process (which I have described in a little more detail below) so your adviser should explain how much they charge for advice, how much they charge for implementation of any product solution (and very often advice and implementation of product solution are bundled together) and how much they charge for any on-going review service, if such a service is required by you.

6. What steps do you take in the process of providing at retirement advice?

This question is designed to provide you with some confidence in the adviser after all you are effectively interviewing them for the job of advising you.

They will go through a typical journey with you. In my firm we refer to this with the acronym EAIR–Engagement, Advice, Implementation, and Review.

The **Engagement** process will encompass asking you a lot of questions about your current financial position, your goals and objectives and your experience of dealing with financial matters.

It will also include ensuring you know what you are going to pay and the services that you will receive in return.

Good advisers usually provide you with an engagement letter setting out services and fees in detail before they start work for you. They will also set out all the important protections that you receive when taking advice from an authorised and regulated adviser.

In delivering **Advice** the adviser will ask you for letters of authority so that they can approach your pension plan provider(s) to gather all the data that they need.

They will then analyse that data and taking into account all that they know about you and your goals and objectives they will construct the advice to you.

This should be in writing and the competent adviser will make sure that they meet with you to go through their advice report so that you have the chance to ask and have answered all of the questions that will inevitably arise.

The advice should contain some specific recommendations about what the adviser believes is most suitable for you.

You are paying for the professional advice of the adviser and whilst outcomes may in many instances be difficult to predict you will want to be confident that what you are being advised to do is best for you and your family.

If the advice leads to a recommendation to take some action your adviser will tell you specifically which product provider and which option or product is right for you.

This **Implementation** process can be quite convoluted so employing an adviser to do this for you can certainly take a lot of the stress out of your life.

You may choose to receive a **Review** service from your adviser and this will be particularly important if your pension pot continues to be invested.

Most of us know that it is the investments that are left alone long enough without review that are most likely to go wrong.

Ask your adviser to describe each of the above steps in as much detail as you feel is appropriate.

7. What information will I have to provide to you?

Most advisers have a standard pro-forma that they use to capture the data that they need. Generically this is known as fact-finding or know your customer. The more information that you can provide to your adviser, the better the likely outcome in respect of the advice they will give you.

Competent advisers are usually skilled at asking questions that will enable you to provide them with all the data that they need both hard and soft facts. How you feel about things can be as important as the basic facts in determining the right outcome for you.

8. What services do you provide in the future?

Whilst the initial challenge is to sort out your pension pot and make the right decisions about what to do now, you may have future requirements from your financial adviser.

It could be that you want to ensure that you manage your estate so that your beneficiaries pay as little inheritance tax in the future as they can. You may also have an eye on the long term future when care planning and the associated fees are required.

Ask your adviser to tell you what else they might be able to do for you in the future.

9. Are you independent in thought about retirement choices and options?

I pose this question because you really want to be dealing with an adviser who has an open mind about the choices and options at retirement. You don't really want to deal with someone who limits their thinking because they have strong prejudices against a particular option, annuity purchase for example.

All of the financial decisions that we make in life have advantages and disadvantages, you will want to work with an adviser who weighs up those advantages and disadvantages and places equal emphasis upon them.

10. What approach do you take to the continued investment of pension pot monies that are not all required at once?

Ask the adviser about their investment philosophy what do they believe is the best way to invest for someone in your position? How often will they carry out reviews of your pension investments and recommend rebalancing and investment fund switching?

How does the adviser choose the investment funds that they recommend? What process do they carry out to select suitable investment funds?

How frequently will they meet with you to review progress to plan because if you are leaving part of your pension pot invested for the future you will probably want a formal review at least yearly.

The Questions to Ask

1. Do you provide independent, impartial advice?

2. What experience do you have in providing at retirement advice?

3. What qualifications do you have in providing at retirement advice?

4. Can you provide me with any references from existing at retirement clients?

5. What are your charges? (Initial fees and on-going service fees)

6. What steps do you take in the process of providing at retirement advice?

7. What information will I have to provide to you?

8. What services do you provide in the future?

9. Are you independent in thought about retirement choices and options?

What approach do you take to the continued investment of pension pot monies that are not all required at once?

Chapter Seven
Your Retirement Budget

Your Retirement Budget

"When can I afford to retire?"

You may remember that I said earlier that is what I hear when people ask me to sort out their pension. The question can only be answered when we know how much is enough.

Use the following pages to build Your Retirement Budget.

Once you have done that, and we know the answers to how much your pension pot will provide, we can start to answer the question, "when can I afford to retire?"

Housekeeping Expenses

Electricity   £
Gas   £
Water Rates   £
Council Tax   £
Home Telephone   £
Repairs & Renewals   £
Solid Fuel   £
Oil   £
Garden/Gardener   £
Help in House   £
House/Contents Ins   £
Other Insurance   £
TV Licence   £
Sky/Digital   £
Internet   £
Other Expenses   £
Alarm   £
Housekeeping/Food   £
Wines & Spirits   £
Laundry/Dry Cleaning   £
Pet Foods   £
Holiday Home   £
Other Expenses   £

Sub Total   £

Personal Expenses

Own Clothing & Footwear	£
Partner's Clothing & Footwear	£
Cigarettes and Tobacco	£
Eating Out	£
Christmas & Birthday Presents	£
Holidays	£
Subscriptions	£
Sports/Hobbies	£
BUPA/PPP/WPA Health Insurance	£
Mobile Phones	£
CDs/Books/Newspapers	£
Miscellaneous spending	£
Gifts to Charities	£
Non Motoring Travel Expenses	£

Sub Total £

Cost of servicing Debts

Mortgage/Loans/Credit Cards	£
Bank Charges	£
Maintenance Payments	£

Sub Total £

Motoring Expenses

Own Car Tax	£
Own Car Insurance	£
Servicing & Repairs	£
AA/RAC Subscription	£
Partners' Car Tax	£
Partners' Car Insurance	£
Petrol & Oil	£
Servicing & Repairs	£
AA/RAC Subscription	£
Sub Total	**£**

Investment and Life Assurance

Life Assurance Premiums	£
Regular Savings Deposits	£
Regular Savings ISAs	£
Other regular savings	£
Sub Total	**£**

Professional Fees

Accountants Fees	£
Dentists Fees	£
Doctors' Fees	£
Opticians Fees	£
Veterinary Fees	£
Sub Total	**£**

Children & Grandchildren Expenses

Type of expense   £

Sub Total   £

Add up all the Sub Total Figures to arrive at a grand total.

Grand Total   £

Chapter Eight
Your Assets

Your Assets

You are about to enter a stage in your life that the financial services profession refers to as a decumulation phase.

This means that instead of building up assets your priority is probably to use those assets to generate income. You may even decide to spend some of your capital or even give it away, possibly to children or grandchildren.

Let's assume though that you need to use those assets to generate additional income to the retirement income you are going to receive from your pension pot. How are you going to do that?

My recommendation is that you consider the following;

Can you afford to spend your asset capital over the next years?

Imagine that you are age 65 and you reckon that your life expectancy is age 85. (Remember how I have said that predicting life expectancy is both important and difficult?) Imagine that you have £100,000 in cash savings

You could simply divide that £100,000 by 20 years and realise that you could spend it at a rate of £5,000 per year to support your retirement lifestyle. Why not do just that?

Well, one reason is that my experience tells me that many people are reluctant to erode their capital in retirement, for many it seems counter intuitive and prompts the response "What if I need it later in life?"

I guess that might generate an answer such as "What if you die before you have spent it all?!"

Think of this as a starting point and ask yourself why you might not spend your capital as if it were income?

- There wouldn't be anything left for my children or grandchildren!

- What if I need to pay for care fees?

- I wouldn't be comfortable having spent all my money.

So don't do it then. Instead think about a different approach.

Continue to save or invest your capital assets and instead take the natural income from the savings or investments. In the case of cash deposits earning interest, the natural income is the net of income tax interest that you receive.

In the case of investments such as stocks and shares ISAs, General Investment Accounts and Investment portfolios, the natural income will be the net of tax dividends, interest and rent (in the case of property) that is generated.

Remember this natural income can go down as well as up in the future (as can the capital itself).

Alternatively you might decide to have a fixed rate of withdrawal regardless of the interest, dividends and rent being generated, in which case if the withdrawal rate is higher than the overall growth rate (income and capital growth) it may still erode your capital but perhaps over a long period of time and you may be more comfortable with that.

I have mentioned taxation but there are two other things that will erode your asset values as well.

The first is inflation which reduces the purchasing power of your money and the second is any management charges that are payable on your savings and investments.

When you work your way through the following chart you need to choose a reasonably robust level of income.

If for example you want a 3% income yield you may have to add 2.5% inflation and say a 1.5% annual management charge so to sustain your capital value in real terms (in excess of inflation) your investments really need to grow at 7% per year.

Put like that you can probably see why you might have to accept some capital erosion over time.

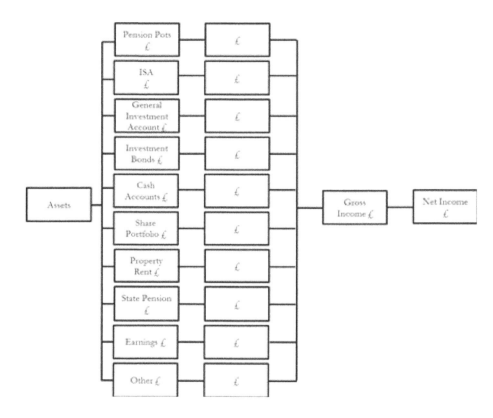

Chapter Nine
Your Action Plan

Your Action Plan

Step one

Read this book. Answer the questions about yourself and ask the questions of your pension pot provider.

Step two

Prepare a retirement budget. How much income will you need to have the retirement lifestyle of your choice?

Step three

Decide if you need to engage with the Citizens Advice Bureau for face-to-face guidance or The Pensions Advisory Service for guidance over the phone.

Alternatively if you feel you need independent and impartial professional advice contact an Independent Financial Adviser.

If you feel confident and want to do-it-yourself, away you go then!

Step four

Decide which of the options you think is best for you.

If you are going to engage with the guidance services ask the person you speak to what they think. Can they see any other advantages or disadvantages that you might have missed?

If you engage with a professional adviser ask them the questions that I have posed in this book. Ask then for a testimonial from a client that they have helped with their at retirement choices and options.

When you feel confident that the adviser you have selected is the right one for you ask them for their engagement terms.

If you decide to do-it-yourself then do some on-line research and find out about the terms that are on offer. If you decide to go directly to a pension product provider, ask then for a key features document and illustration.

Step five

Arrange for the transfer of your pension pot monies into the plan that is going to provide you with your retirement benefits, or hand this task over to your selected financial adviser to complete.

Step six

Make a note of any other assets that you have and the likely level of income that they might produce and add this to the income that you are going to receive from your pension pot.

Compare this total with the expenditure that you have identified in your retirement budget planning.

Step seven

Enjoy the fact that you have arrived at a desired outcome and no longer have to stress about what to do with your pension pot.

Well done!

Lightning Source UK Ltd.
Milton Keynes UK
UKOW06f1304171115

262912UK00018B/586/P

9 781326 145903